BROMSGROVE
TO
GLOUCESTER

Vic Mitchell and Keith Smith

MP *Middleton Press*

Cover picture: A Birmingham to Gloucester local train departs from Ashchurch on 6th September 1952, headed by class 8F 2-8-0 no. 48417. (Millbrook House)

Published February 2006

ISBN 1 904474 73 X

Design Deborah Esher

Published by
>   *Middleton Press*
>   *Easebourne Lane*
>   *Midhurst, West Sussex*
>   *GU29 9AZ*
Tel: 01730 813169
Fax: 01730 812601
Email: info@middletonpress.co.uk
www.middletonpress.co.uk

Printed & bound by Biddles Ltd, Kings Lynn

INDEX

ACKNOWLEDGEMENTS

We are very grateful for the assistance received from many of those mentioned in the credits also to P.G.Barnes, W.R.Burton, A.R.Carder, L.Crosier, G.Croughton, M.Dart, J.Gardner, T.Hancock, F.Hornby, N.Langridge, B.W.Leslie, Mr D. and Dr S.Salter, R.E.Toop and particularly our ever supportive wives, Barbara Mitchell and Janet Smith.

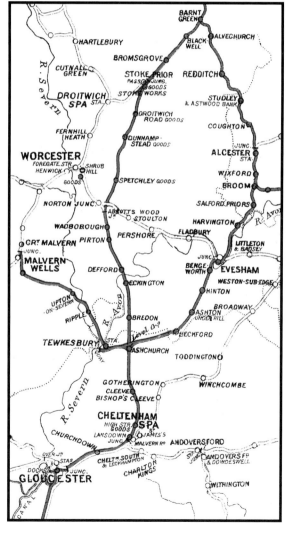

I.   Railway Clearing House map for 1947. The solid lines are LMSR and the hollow ones GWR.

GEOGRAPHICAL SETTING

Bromsgrove is at the foot of the Lickey Hills, on the southern fringe of the Birmingham conurbation. The line falls fairly steadily from 270ft above sea level to 70ft at Ashchurch. The first five miles are on Keuper Marl and the remainder of the main line traverses Lower Lias Limestone. It is not close to any major waterways, except the River Avon at Defford.

However, the Malvern branch had an intimate relationship with the River Severn, crossing it at both Tewkesbury and Upton. West of the latter it climbed gently to the foot of the Malvern Hills at the famous spa town of Malvern Wells.

The southern section of the main line is in the widening Severn Valley as it passes close to the much larger spa town of Cheltenham on its way to Gloucester, historically the lowest crossing point of the River Severn. Of Roman origin, the city is noted for its fine cathedral and once busy docks, now given over to pleasure boating.

Tewkesbury and Ashchurch are in the northern part of Gloucestershire, the route north thereof being in Worcestershire.

The maps are to the scale of 25ins to 1 mile, with north at the top, unless otherwise indicated.

II. Gradient profile showing the mileage from the Midland Railway's headquarters at Derby.

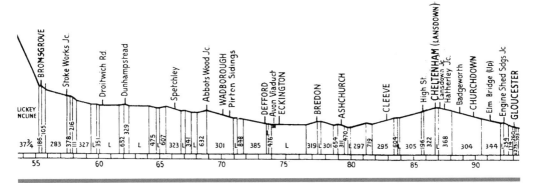

HISTORICAL BACKGROUND

The Cheltenham & Gloucester Railway was a 3ft 6ins gauge plateway which began operation in 1810. This tramway terminated at Gloucester Docks and ceased operation in 1859. The first conventional line in the area was the Birmingham & Gloucester Railway, which opened to passengers between Bromsgrove and Cheltenham on 24th June 1840 and between Cheltenham and Gloucester on 4th November 1840. It was standard gauge and became part of the Midland Railway on 7th May 1845.

The Great Western Railway between Bath and Bristol opened on 31st August 1840. It was broad gauge and was completed to London in June 1841. The Cheltenham & Great Western Union Railway was laid to the broad gauge of 7ft 0¼ins and opened to Swindon on 8th July 1844, the same day as the Bristol & Gloucester Railway, which was of the same gauge. It was expected that both routes would become part of the GWR, but the Midland Railway offered a higher figure for the latter and took over

its operation on 7th May 1845, together with the Birmingham & Gloucester.

The Cheltenham-Gloucester section was jointly owned and mixed gauge initially. From 1867, it was divided halfway instead, an arrangement that persisted until 1948.

A branch from Ashchurch to Tewkesbury was opened by the Birmingham & Gloucester Railway on 21st July 1840. It was horse worked until 18th February 1844.

The South Wales Railway reached Gloucester on 19th September 1851 and it became part of the GWR in 1862. The MR was otherwise standard gauge and so it converted its line to Bristol on 22nd May 1854.

A branch from the MR main line to Worcester opened on 5th October 1850, although the track belonged to the Oxford, Worcester & Wolverhampton Railway, which itself did not open until 1852, apart from its northern extremity. It included a line between

Droitwich Spa and Stoke Works, on the MR main line. This allowed long distance MR trains to travel via Worcester. The OWWR became part of the West Midland Railway in 1860 and the GWR in 1863.

The Tewkesbury & Malvern Railway opened on 16th May 1864, although the one mile north of Malvern Wells to the junction with the 1860 Worcester-Hereford line had come into use on 1st July 1862. The TMR became part of the MR in 1877. The main line through Malvern was GWR property from 1863. The MR branch from Ashchurch to Evesham saw traffic from 1864. The broad gauge lines south from Cheltenham were not used after 1872.

Closures took place thus:

	Passengers	Goods
Upton to Malvern	1952	1952
Tewkesbury to Upton	1961	1963
Ashchurch to Tewkesbury	1961	1964
Ashchurch to Evesham	1963	1963
Cheltenham towards Banbury	1962	1962
Cheltenham towards Stratford	1960	1977

Precise dates are given in the relevant captions, as are closures of intermediate stations and goods depots.

As a consequence of privatisation, trains on

The Banbury & Cheltenham Direct Railway arrived in Cheltenham in 1877 and became a constituent of the GWR in 1897. A triangular junction, south of the town, was created in 1906, the year in which the GWR opened a line from Cheltenham to Stratford-upon-Avon.

The MR became part of the London Midland & Scottish Railway (LMS) on 1st January 1923, which mostly became the London Midland Region of British Railways upon nationalisation in 1948. Our route and its branches were transferred to the Western Region on 1st February 1958.

the route were operated by Virgin CrossCountry from March 1997 and also by Central Trains, but most of these were routed via Worcester.

PASSENGER SERVICES

The figures in brackets apply to Sundays. The 1850 timetable showed six (3) departures south from Bromsgrove. They called at all stations, except for four trains which omitted four minor stops.

By 1869 there were ten (2) down trains, but most intermediate stations were served by only three of them. A similar pattern applied 20 years later, but in 1909 there were 16 (4). Most local stations saw only five (2) trains stop.

A further 20 years on and the departures numbered seven (5), but the southern part of the route had more local trains originating at Worcester, while Bromsgrove had more terminating there. There was also an increase in the number of through expresses.

The year 1949 showed a reduction to five (3) to accommodate long distance and freight train increases. There were few stopping trains over the entire route. Nearing the end of local trains in 1963, the timetable showed all but one of the stopping services operating via Worcester, but a change was often needed there. There were five (0), all-stations trains south thereof.

Following the decline of local services, the general pattern has been for long distance trains

to speed along the entire length of the route and to bypass Gloucester, while the others have served both Worcester and Gloucester. Thus Cheltenham receives all trains, plus a dedicated London service.

Ashchurch - Great Malvern

The table summarises the weekday train frequencies in 20 year intervals, but omits Saturday-only services, also others on single days.

	Ashchurch-Tewkesbury	Tewkesbury - Great Malvern
1869	4	4
1889	10	4
1909	14	4
1929	9	5
1949	6	3

Following closure of the northern section in 1952, Upton-on-Severn received one train in the early morning and another in the evening, while Tewkesbury had four more. This service lasted to the end.

We have found no evidence of Sunday trains.

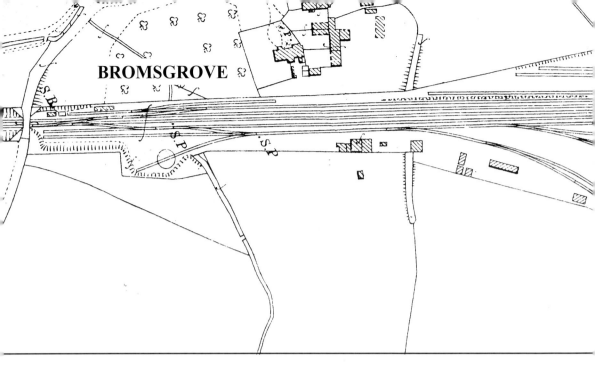

BROMSGROVE

III.   The 1901 survey has the line to Gloucester on the left; this was quadrupled to Stoke Works Junction in 1932-33. The saw mill is near the group of four wagon turntables. The premises had been the BGR loco works until the MR takeover. In the 1870s, there were about 600 employees. Upon closure in 1964, there were over 200.

1.   The designation "up" applies from Gloucester to Bromsgrove and no. 3696 is running in that direction on 12th July 1939. It is facing the Lickey Incline, which is at 1 in 37. The LMS inherited an amazing 1598 0-6-0s from the MR. The line on the left was removed in 1969 and a new platform was built later. (H.C.Casserley)

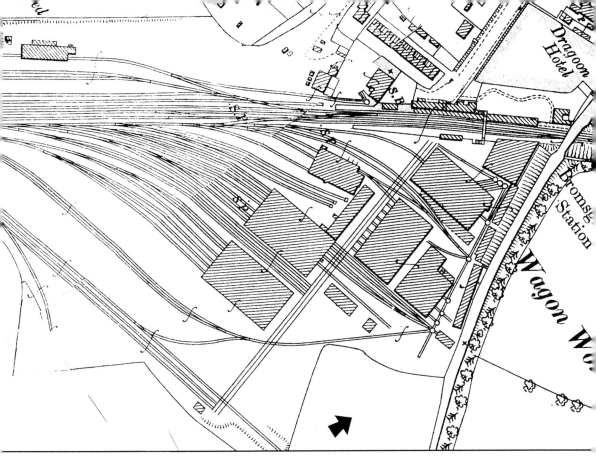

2.   Speeding south in July 1949 is 4-6-0 "Jubilee" class no. 45658 *Keyes*. On the left is the goods crane, which was rated at five tons, and the engine shed is on the right. A private siding for Deritend Stamping had been added on the up side in about 1942. (Millbrook House)

3.   A closer view of the loco depot in 1949 includes the wagon works in the background and features class 3F 0-6-0T no. 7234, one of eight of this type used for assisting trains up the wwLickey Incline. The shed closed on 27th September 1964; its code was 21C from 1934, 85F from 1958 and 85D from 1961. (H.C.Casserley)

4. The view towards Birmingham in September 1958 includes Station box, which had 36 levers and closed in 1969. This and the other railway buildings were subsequently destroyed. (H.C.Casserley)

5. A July 1959 photograph reveals the details of the improvements to the shed, when compared with picture 3. The Pannier tanks were regarded as invaders at this ex-LMS depot. The tower on the right was the water softener plant. (R.S.Carpenter)

6.   No. 46029 is northbound on 15th September 1975 and is level with the 1969 replacement ticket office. Only the up platform was in use for a period. The goods yard had closed on 5th June 1967, but some sidings were retained to serve an oil depot. In 2005, there were five sidings and two goods loops, the down one continuing to Stoke Works Junction. (T.Heavyside)

7.   The driver of no. 66055 is changing ends before crossing to the down sidings on 4th November 2005. Also evident is the steepness of Lickey Incline and the paucity of passenger shelter. The basic service was an hourly DMU between Droitwich Spa and Nottingham. (V.Mitchell)

SOUTH OF BROMSGROVE

8.   This 1954 panorama is from the road bridge on the left of the map and has the goods shed and station in the background. The coal stage was for Lickey banking engines, the one nearest being the 0-10-0 described in the next caption. Lower left is the tray for ash from smokeboxes. In the left background is Garrington's rail-served factory. (J.Moss/R.S.Carpenter)

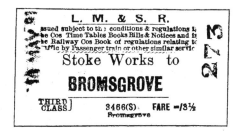

9.　　　Nearer the bridge there had been a conveyor to aid coaling. It is seen in July 1949 in the company of the unique ex-MR 0-10-0, unofficially named *Big Bertha*. Built in 1919 specially for banking north hereof, it is fitted with a headlight. It was withdrawn in 1956 and replaced by BR class 9F 2-10-0 no. 92079. (Millbrook House)

10.　　　The connections on the left of this picture are on the right of photograph no. 8. BR 4-6-0 no. 73046 is working a special from Bournville to Salisbury on 11th May 1956. The 60-lever South Box was in use from 1922 until 1969. There was a turntable behind it until 1964. (T.J.Edgington)

STOKE WORKS JUNCTION

IV.   The route to Droitwich Spa and Worcester is is upper left on the left of this 1901 extract.
There are several sidings running into the salt works, the double track passing over the
Worcester & Birmingham Canal. A works was started in 1825 west of the canal, where
the salt was mined. Another firm built a works east of the waterway following borings.
Private sidings were authorised in 1845 and the two works were operated as one
by John Corbett by 1857. A Manning Wardle 0-4-0ST was purchased in 1875
and named *Raven*. Following in 1883 was *Elephant*, a Hawthorn 0-4-0ST.
Salt Union Ltd took over in 1888 and four more 0-4-0STs followed.
There was a fleet of 400 vans and wagons by that time. Production
also included soap, alkalis, metallic sulphates and sulphuric
acid. ICI bought the works in 1937 and eventually used
diesel engines for shunting, changing to road tractors in
1962. Rail traffic ceased in 1964 and salt production
ended in 1972, partly due to fear of subsidence
in the Droitwich area. Left of centre is the
signal box, which is mentioned in caption
12. The line to Droitwich was singled
in December 1964.

S.P.

S.P.

S.B.

P.

S.B.

ice

S.P.

S.P.

Stoke Prior S

F.B.

STOKE WORKS

V.   This map is a continuation of the previous one, but is a little further south. The first station opened with the BGR and was sited near the goods shed. It closed on 1st October 1855 and was burnt down in 1929. The one marked came into use in 1853. Both were shown in the MR timetables in 1854. Until that time, there was an omnibus service to Worcester. Ownership was OWWR, WMR and then GWR, until 1948. However, up to that time staff and equipment were provided by the LMS, although the last two station masters were GWR men.

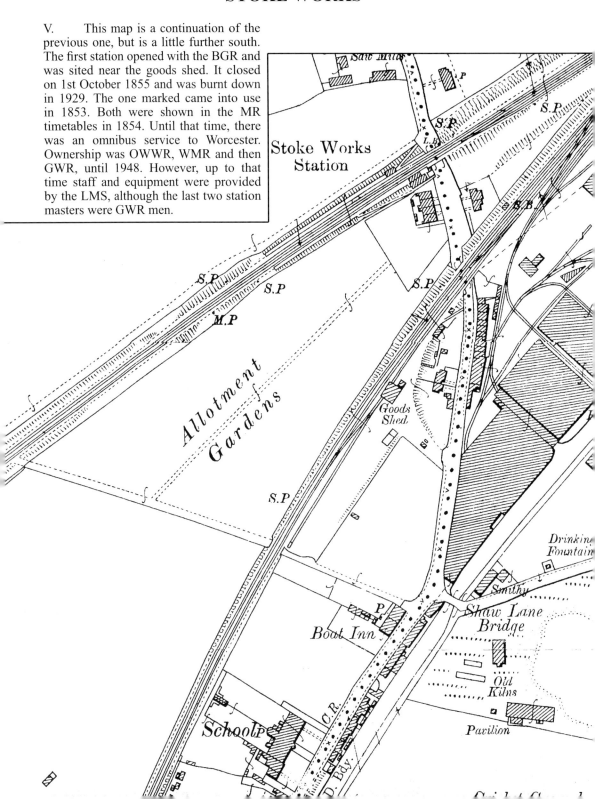

11.   The humid atmosphere in and around the works was notoriously unpleasant. Three open wagons have probably delivered coal; the roofs of two vans are visible. These were no doubt for conveyance of the finished products, which included table salt. (Droitwich Spa Town Council)

12.   Goods traffic ceased on 1st June 1964 and passenger service was withdrawn on 18th April 1966. The station was in the parish of Stoke Prior and this name appears on some railway maps. This is the view towards Bromsgrove in April 1964, with part of the chemical works on the right. Latex production started here in 1961. The shelter obscures the signal box, which had 65 levers and closed on 10th March 1969. In the final timetable, one train called here on Mondays to Fridays only. (R.G.Nelson/T.Walsh)

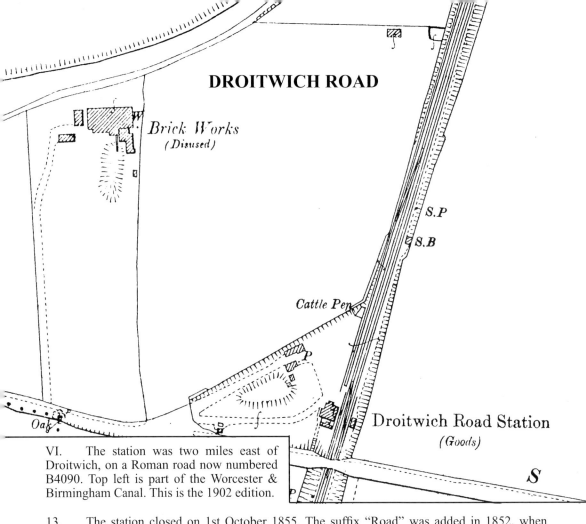

DROITWICH ROAD

Brick Works
(Disused)

S.P

S.B

Cattle Pen

P

Oak

Droitwich Road Station
(Goods)

S

VI.   The station was two miles east of Droitwich, on a Roman road now numbered B4090. Top left is part of the Worcester & Birmingham Canal. This is the 1902 edition.

13.   The station closed on 1st October 1855. The suffix "Road" was added in 1852, when Droitwich Spa station opened. The brickworks is in the background in this view from the road bridge in about 1920. Goods traffic continued until 1st October 1952. (Lens of Sutton coll.)

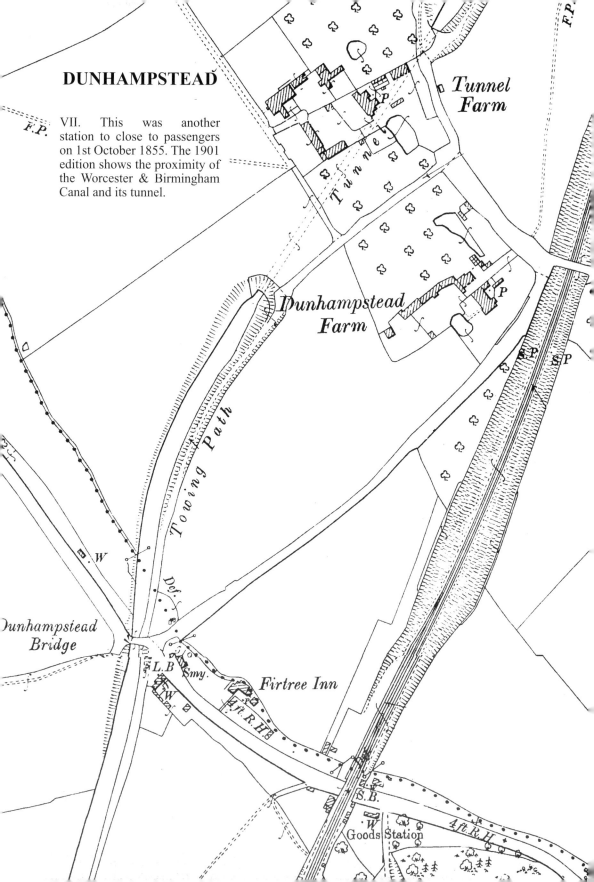

DUNHAMPSTEAD

VII. This was another station to close to passengers on 1st October 1855. The 1901 edition shows the proximity of the Worcester & Birmingham Canal and its tunnel.

Tunnel Farm

Tunnel

Dunhampstead Farm

Towing Path

Dunhampstead Bridge

Firtree Inn

Goods Station

14. Three photographs from May 1974 show all that remained at that time. The goods yard had closed on 1st October 1949, but the single siding was not removed until about 1955. This is the yard office and the staff house. (R.S.Carpenter)

——————▶

15. The signal box ceased to be a block post on 10th March 1969 and the crossover was then taken out of use. The box had opened on 13th July 1886. (R.S.Carpenter)

——————▶

16. The white levers are all out of use, but the wheel still worked the gates over a minor road to Huddington. Half a mile to the south, the box at Oddingley was still doing that in 2005, but it was not a block post either. (R.S.Carpenter)

3rd-SINGLE SINGLE-3rd
Eckington to
Eckington   Eckington
Defford   Defford
DEFFORD
(W)   4d   FARE   4d   (W
For conditions see over For conditions see over

5355   5355
3388   3388

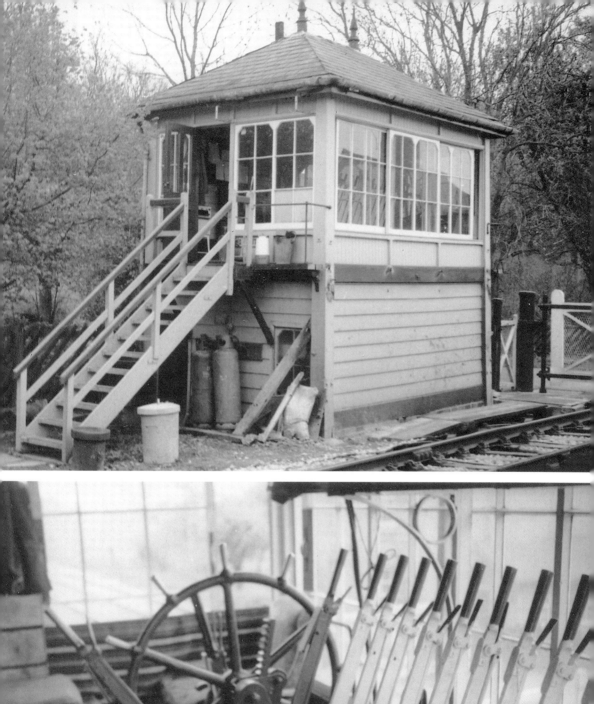

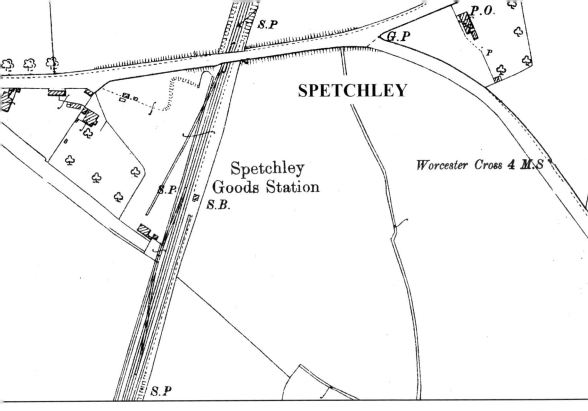

SPETCHLEY

Spetchley
Goods Station
S.B.

Worcester Cross **4 M.S**

VIII.   The 1904 survey includes the 30-lever signal box and the sidings, which were in use until 2nd January 1961. The bridge now carries the A422. About 2½ miles to the south is Abbots Wood Junction for the Worcester line. Its 35-lever signal box closed on 8th March 1969.

17.   This is a further station to lose its passenger service on 1st October 1855. It had a siding (in use until 1961), a down goods loop, a signal box until 1969 and an up goods loop, which was still functional in 2005. The building was at 90° to the main line and was recorded in 1950. Abbots Wood Junction passenger operation was equally short lived. (RCHS)

WADBOROUGH

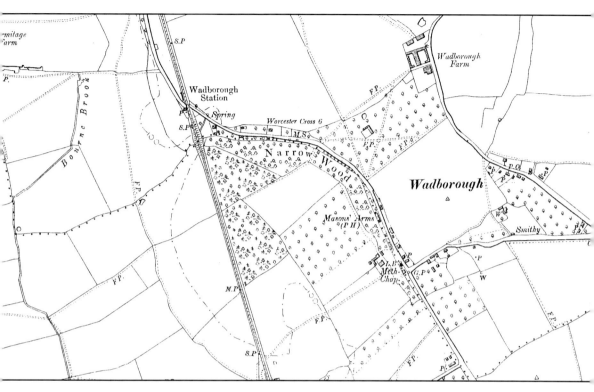

IX.   The 1938 map at 6ins to 1 mile emphasises the low population density of the area and that orchards were numerous.

18.   Timber framed and timber clad, the buildings were similar to those on the up side at Berkeley Road and were well suited to such a rural paradise. This is also the up side and was photographed on 31st August 1960. (H.B.Priestley/Milepost 92½)

19.   Seen on the same day is no. 45654 *Hood* speeding towards its destination of Sheffield. Local trains were withdrawn on 4th January 1965. (H.B.Priestley/Milepost 92½)

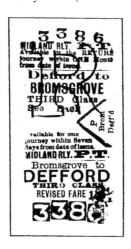

PIRTON

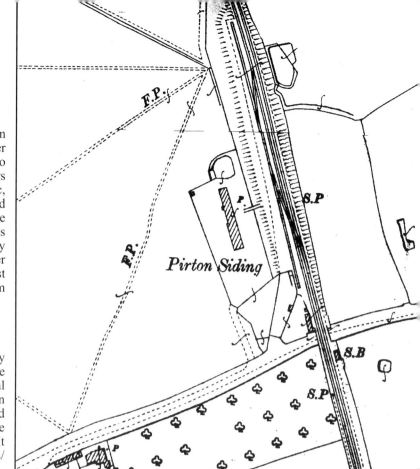

X. The station opened in November 1841 and closed to passengers three years later. Goods traffic, however, continued until 1st July 1963. The next station south was Besford, but it was only open from November 1841 to about August 1846. The map is from 1904.

Pirton Siding

20. By 1960, the only structure of note here was Pirton Sidings signal box, which opened on 15th October 1933 and became a ground frame on 10th March 1969. It had 20 levers. (J.Moss/R.S.Carpenter)

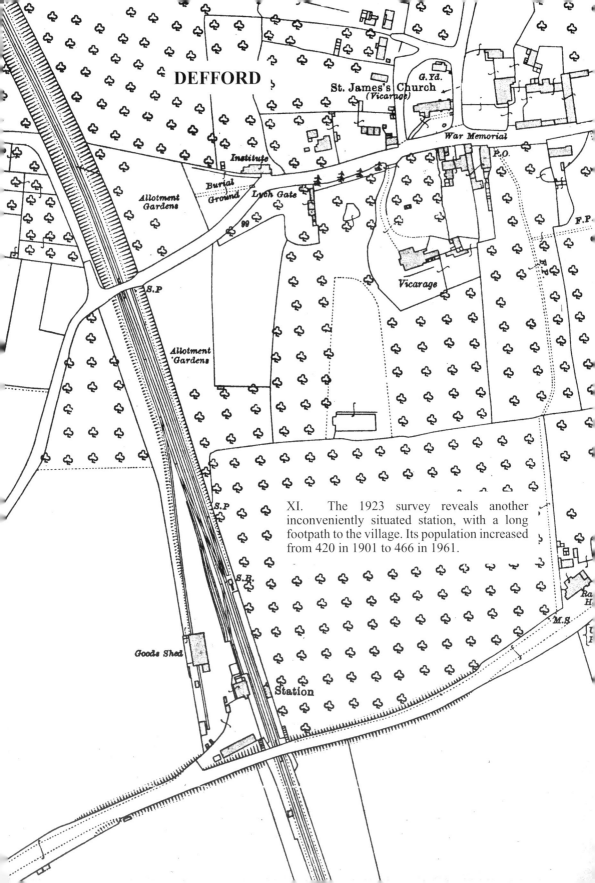

DEFFORD

St. James's Church
(Vicarage)

G.Yd.

War Memorial

P.O.

Institute

Burial
Ground

Lych Gate

Allotment
Gardens

F.P.

99

F.P.

S.P

Vicarage

Allotment
Gardens

S.P

XI. The 1923 survey reveals another
inconveniently situated station, with a long
footpath to the village. Its population increased
from 420 in 1901 to 466 in 1961.

S.B.

M.S.

Goods Shed

Station

21.   A postcard view from the road bridge in about 1912 shows the goods yard to be full to capacity. Included are a lime-washed cattle wagon attached to a horsebox, plus a trap and a goods cart. (Lens of Sutton coll.)

22.   The flower beds were still neatly tended in the 1920s. The down waiting shelter has been repositioned when compared with the previous view. There had earlier been a water column in the right foreground. (Stations UK)

23. Unconventionally, there were no doors onto the platform. Being amongst the earliest stations in the land, a convention had not been established when it was built. It is seen from a down train in May 1956. (H.C.Casserley)

24. The 16-lever signal box closed on 3rd May 1964; the down refuge siding beyond it in this 1960 view is overgrown, but was usable until June 1963. Local freight ceased on 1st July 1963 and passenger services ended on 4th January 1965. (H.B.Priestley/Milepost 92½)

SOUTH OF DEFFORD

25.   An engraving from about 1850 gives an impression of the elaborate structure required to cross the River Avon. The next railway crossing upstream is at Pershore. (C.G.Maggs coll.)

26.   The bridge was rebuilt between April and July 1931, one side at a time with a temporary signal box for single line working. On the 73yd long structure on 4th August 1989 is a pair of class 37 diesels with a southbound train of steel. (M.Turvey)

ECKINGTON

XII. The 1923 survey indicates the close proximity of the village centre to the station and that it was in a fruit growing area. There were 651 inhabitants in 1901 and 803 in 1961.

27. Our survey uses three photos from the 1950s. This northward view features the signal box, which had 24 levers and ceased to be a block post in February 1969, but it continued to control the gates until December 1972. (R.M.Casserley)

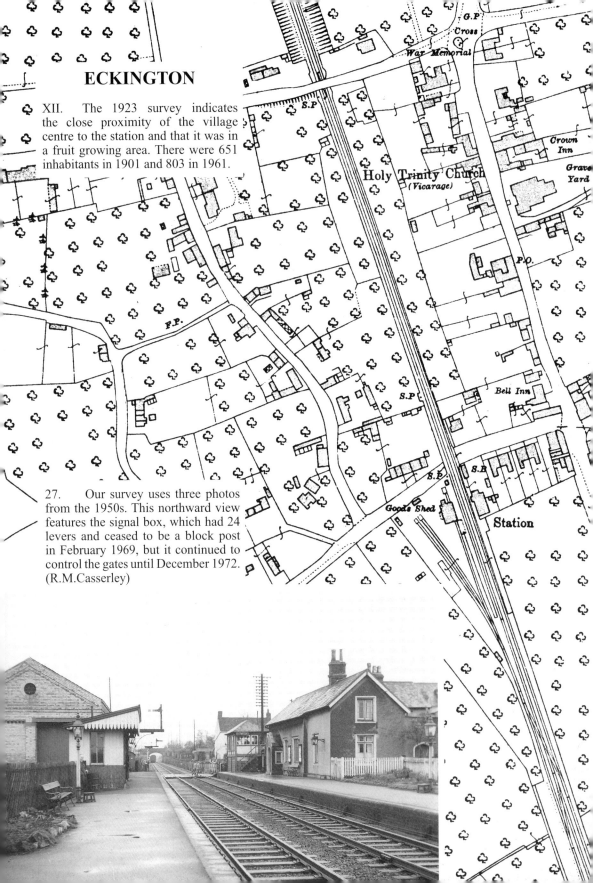

G.P
Cross
War Memorial
Crown Inn
Holy Trinity Church
(Vicarage)
Grave Yard
S.P.
S.P
P.O.
F.P.
Bell Inn
S.P.
S.B
S.B
Goods Shed
Station

28.   Looking south, we see the long up goods loop, which was formed from a refuge siding in 1942 and was still in place in 2005. On the right are the lines to the goods yard, which was in use until 1st October 1951. Passenger service was also withdrawn that day. (J.Moss/R.S.Carpenter)

29.   This was recorded as the second station and was listed as opening on 13th September 1874. This would explain its conventional orientation. (H.C.Casserley)

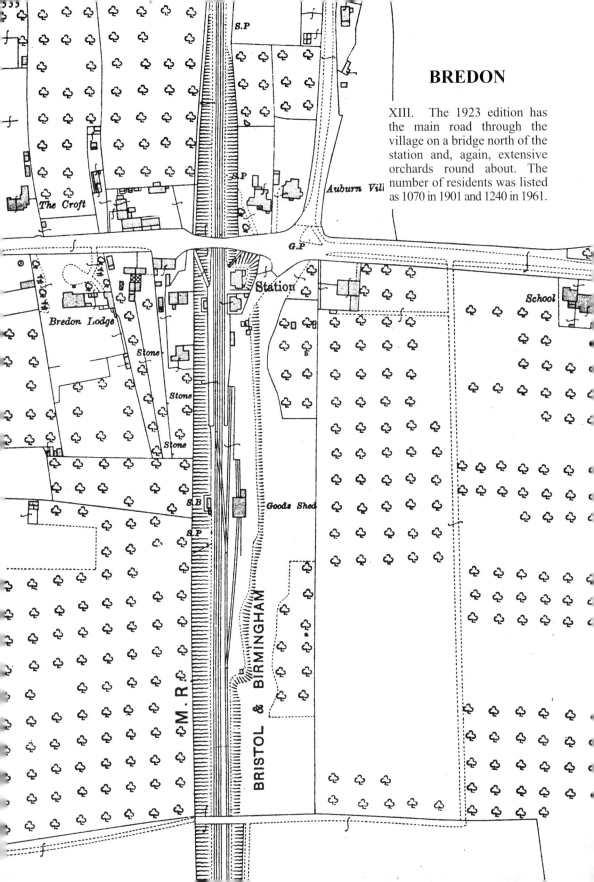

BREDON

XIII.   The 1923 edition has the main road through the village on a bridge north of the station and, again, extensive orchards round about. The number of residents was listed as 1070 in 1901 and 1240 in 1961.

30.   The steps down from the road are evident in this postcard view from about 1912, as is a MR nameboard. Beyond the bridge is the lower arm of coacting signals, required because of the sighting restrictions caused by the bridge visible in the distance in the next picture. (Lens of Sutton coll.)

31.   We can now enjoy four views from the 1950s. This includes the black diagonal fencing, so widely a feature of MR stations. Empty fruit boxes scattered near the parcels shed are a reminder of this important traffic. (J.Moss/R.S.Carpenter)

32. An additional building became necessary on the down side and it included a booking office. Other examples of this polychromatic herring-bone brickwork could be found on the Malvern branch. (J.Moss/R.S.Carpenter)

33. This southward panorama includes more fruit boxes. The goods yard closed on 1st July 1963 and the signal box lasted until 17th February 1969. (J.Moss/R.S.Carpenter)

34.   Taken from the slope down from the highway, this picture includes the unusual chimney of the up side waiting room and reveals that the parcels shed was formed of a van body. (H.C.Casserley)

35.   The up waiting room is visible in detail as 0-6-0 no. 44167 plods north with a pick-up freight on 17th August 1960. Passenger service ceased here on 4th January 1965. The station was gaslit to the end. (H.B.Priestley/Milepost 92½)

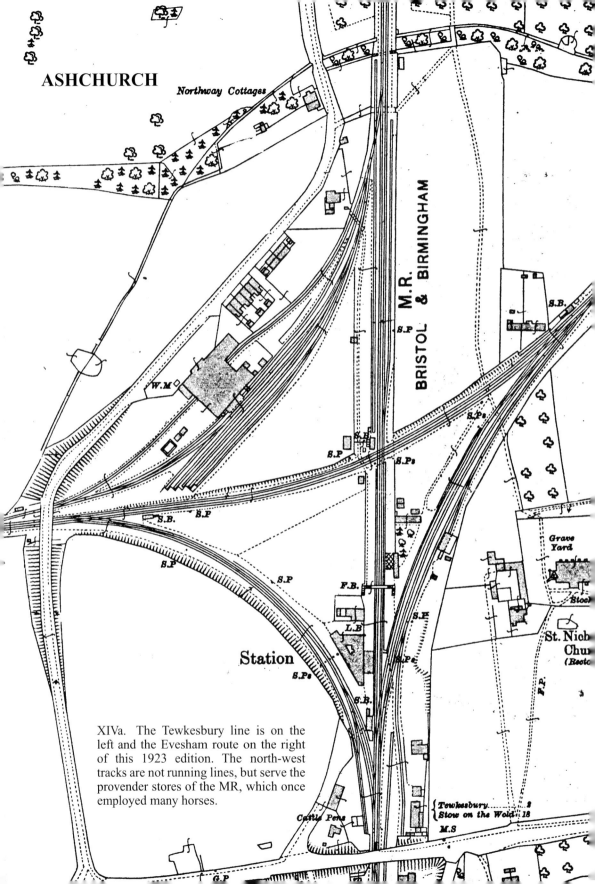

ASHCHURCH

Northway Cottages

W.M

BRISTOL & BIRMINGHAM M.R.

S.B.

S.P

S.P

S.Ps

S.Ps

S.P

S.B.

S.P

S.P

S.P

S.P

S.Ps

Station

S.Ps

F.B.

L.B

S.P

S.Ps

S.B.

Grave Yard

Stoc

St. Nich Chu (Recto

F.P.

XIVa. The Tewkesbury line is on the left and the Evesham route on the right of this 1923 edition. The north-west tracks are not running lines, but serve the provender stores of the MR, which once employed many horses.

Cattle Pens

{ *Tewkesbury* 2
{ *Stow on the Wold* .. 18
M.S

G.P.

36.   A postcard view north from the main road has the Bromsgrove line in the centre, in about 1910. There are several MR wagons on the right and the cattle dock is in the left foreground. (Brunel University/Clinker coll.)

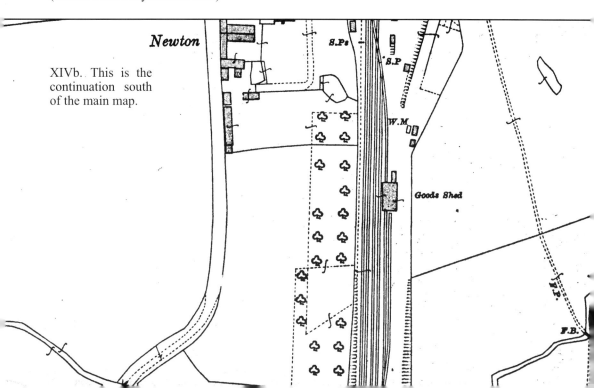

Newton

XIVb. This is the continuation south of the main map.

Goods Shed

37.   This fine study of no. 41097 departing with a Birmingham to Gloucester local train in 1949 shows that there was a siding parallel to the main line. This was in use for military traffic in 2005, to and from a depot close to the stub of the Evesham line. (J.Moss/R.S.Carpenter)

38.   No. 3507 runs north on 9th September 1949 and passes under the curiously designed footbridge. Trains of this great length and variety were fascinating features of the railway scene up to the 1960s. (H.C.Casserley)

39.   The 2.45pm Worcester to Bristol was recorded on the same day, with a horsebox behind 4-4-0 no. 41047. The signal box dates from before 1927 and was called "Ashchurch Level Crossing". (H.C.Casserley)

40.   A few minutes later and class 4P 2-6-4T no. 42326 ran over the main line, while turning on the triangle; the reason for the box name becomes apparent. (H.C.Casserley)

41.   A southward view of the goods yard on 6th September 1952 includes 0-4-4T no. 58071 with several cattle wagons. This area is on map XIVb. Local goods service was withdrawn on 1st June 1964, but most of the sidings were still in place in 2005. The large pipes on the boiler were for steam condensing when the locomotive worked underground in London. (Millbrook House)

42.   No. 43046 runs east over the level crossing on 21st March 1957, as youngsters wander near the water tank and a porter waits by a Sugg's Rochester pattern gas lamp. The single line was lifted in 1957; it had been double until about 1927. (T.J.Edgington)

43.	The MR used vaulted roofs widely, but seldom just two spans alone and at such great height. The goods shed is in the background. (R.M.Casserley)

44.	The Tewkesbury platform was devoid of shelter and was very wide. No. 41900 is arriving with a train from Upton-on-Severn on 23rd August 1958. The line to Tewkesbury was singled in about June 1958 and one track was used for wagon storage thereafter. (E.Wilmshurst)

45.	No. 41900 is seen again after arrival with a branch train, this time on 7th March 1959. Behind it is the cattle dock, while on the right is the approach road. The building adjacent to it is probably the stable block, which would have housed the initial motive power for the branch. (G.Adams/M.J.Stretton)

46.	Another Tewkesbury train was recorded, this time the 9.40am departure on 1st October 1960. Station staffing ceased on 14th September 1970. Western Region locomotives were in use after 1958; this is 0-6-0PT no. 97700. (H.C.Casserley)

47.   A northbound express from Bristol roars through in about 1962, hauled by no. 45690 *Leander*, one of the three "Jubilee" class locos to be preserved. Included is the new signal box, which opened on 27th July 1958, but closed on 17th February 1969. It had 101 levers. The station lasted longer than the others, closing on 15th November 1971. (J.Moss/R.S.Carpenter)

48.   The curves in the right background are those seen on the right of photo 36, but they lead only to Ashchurch MOD Depot. The water tank in picture 40 is in the background, but no other relics remained. The line in the right foreground was added in 1961 to make connection with the goods yard. No. 47853 is heading the 09.30 Wolverhampton to Exeter on 2nd May 1993. (M.Turvey)

49.   The folly of closure was rectified on 30th May 1997, when two new platforms were opened. A new approach road and an extensive car park were provided on the west side. The name "Ashchurch for Tewkesbury" was applied. The Virgin Voyager is working the 07.05 Leeds to Plymouth on 11th August 2005. (C.G.Maggs)

L. M. & S. R.
FOR CONDITIONS SEE NOTICES

BREDON   TO
ASHCHURCH

THIRD
CLASS]   3507 (S   FARE -/5 C
            ASHCHURCH

6243

L. M. & S. R.
Issued subject to the conditions & regulations in the Cos Time Tables Books Bills & Notices and in the Railway Cos Book of regulations relating to traffic by Passenger train or other similar service

ECKINGTON(B.&B.) TO
BREDON

THIRD
CLASS]   3506(S)   FARE -/4½
            BREDON

1862

DOWTY

50.   Dowty Hydraulic Units Ltd created an area for testing buffing and drawgear, near the bridge shown on the left of the map. On the right is a retarder and in the background the Tewkesbury line is seen in about 1958. (C.G.Maggs coll.)

51.   Dowty Engineering took over the former provender store and retained the sidings from the north. This 1962 view is northeast from the road bridge just seen and has the Tewkesbury line lower right. (J.Moss/R.S.Carpenter)

52.   The Dowty Railway Preservation Society was formed in 1962 and it involved many employees. A two-foot operational line was established and Kerr Stuart 0-4-0ST *Peter Pan* was in steam on the last public open day, 25th September 1982. (T.Heavyside)

53.   *Peter Pan* is on one of its last runs on the site; it has subsequently spent most of its time on the Leighton Buzzard Railway. Most of the remaining equipment was moved to a site adjacent to the Gloucestershire & Warwickshire Railway's nearby Toddington station, where it operates as the North Gloucestershire Railway; see our *Stratford-upon-Avon to Cheltenham* album, pictures 68 and 69. (T.Heavyside)

54.   The standard gauge stock did not go to Toddington. Running close to the main line (near the top of the map) on the last day of the system is Avonside 0-4-0T no. 1977 of 1925 in the livery of its previous owner. It now resides at Tyseley Locomotive Works. (T.Heavyside)

Malvern Branch
TEWKESBURY

XV. The first station was situated between the two streets on the left, High Street and The Oldbury. It was in use by passengers until 16th May 1864, when the one on the right page came into use. The line on the left of this 1901 edition continued over the River Avon to serve two mills and a loop on the quay. The loop at Quay Street was used by Tewkesbury Brewery. The crane shown near the goods shed was rated at five tons. The scale is 22ins to 1 mile. The town had been granted the status of a port in the 16th century and was subsequently noted for boat building, milling and weaving.

55. This is the west end of the first station in July 1934. The line between the High Street and the quay was lifted in December 1957. (Mowat coll./Brunel University)

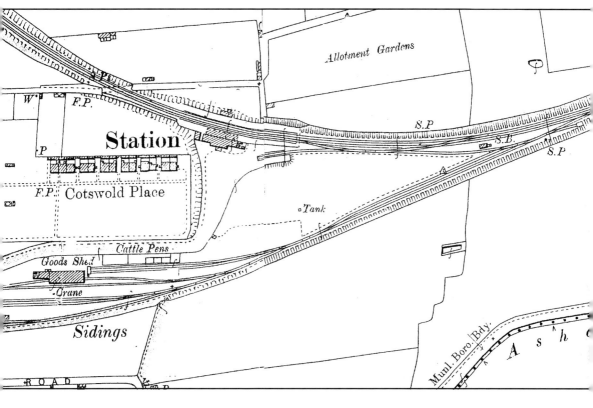

56.　A photo from the same viewpoint in February 1953 shows the extent of the former passenger platform. No. 45265 is reversing at the points near The Oldbury crossing, the locomotive shed being in the distance. (R.M.Casserley coll.)

57. A close look at the engine shed on 9th September 1949 shows it to be attached to the malthouse - see map. The locomotive is class 3F 0-6-0 no. 43506. The track in this area was not used after 7th September 1962, when the shed closed. It was in industrial use until demolished in 1986. (H.C.Casserley)

ASHCHURCH, TEWKESBURY, and MALVERN.—Midland.

Miles		mrn	mrn	mrn	mrn	mrn	aft	aft	aft	aft	aft	aft
	Temple Mead,											
	Bristol 276 dep	....	7 35	....	1015	1055	12½	1 15	3 50	....	5 0	7 0
	276 Cheltenham ‖	7 54	9 20	....	1139	1250	1550	3 49	4 54	....	7 1	8 28
	Ashchurch....dep	8 27	9 45	1014	1210	1 15	2 15	4 10	5 15	6 25	7 33	8 55
1½	Tewkesbury......	8 35	9 50	1020	1215	1 21	2 20	4 15	5 20	6 30	7 38	9 0
5½	Ripple..................	....	10 2	....	....	1 30	....	5 29	....	7 46	....
7¼	Upton-on-Severn	....	10 8	....	....	1 36	....	5 36	....	7 52	....
11½	Malvern Wells *	....	1017	....	....	1 49	....	5 44	....	8 3	....
14	Gt. Malvern 32, 33	....	1025	....	....	1 55	....	5 55	....	8 10	....
—	274 Hereford† arr	....	1155	....	....	3 34	....	7 35	....	....
—	274 ‖ (Barr's C.)‖	....	1155	....	....	3 30	....	7 33	....	....
—	Worcester 33 ‖	....	1113	....	....	3 5	....	6 34	....	9 20	....

Miles		mrn	mrn	mrn	mrn	aft	aft	aft	aft	aft	aft
	Shrub Hill,										
	32 Worcester dp	....	7 35	....	1025	....	2	5	....	5 40	....
	276 Hereford†.‖	....	....	....	9 35	....	1235	....	5 15	....
	276 ‖ (Bartn) ‖	....	....	....	9 27	....	1232	....	....
	Great Malvrn.dp	....	8 25	....	1110	....	3 10	....	6 35	....
	Malvern Wells..	....	8 32	....	1119	....	3 16	....	6 42	....
	Upton-on-Severn	....	8 42	....	1129	....	3 25	....	6 53	....
	Ripple ....[273	....	8 48	....	1136	....	3 31	....	7 0	....
	Tewkesbry [276,	8 58	8 59	55	1146	1255	1 55	3 39	4 50	5 7	10 8	35
	Ashchurch 275,	8 11	9	6	10 1	1152	1 2	1 3	4 54	56	11 7	18	8 41
	275 Cheltnhm.ar	....	9 33	1019	1220	....	2 20	4 5	5c16	6 30	7 51	1018
	Bristol 275 ‖	....	1140	1150	2 5	....	3 40	5 25	....	7 50	1135	1135

* Hanley Road Station; about 1½ mile to The Common Station, Great Western Railway.   † Barton Station.   ‡ Barr's Court.

May 1889

UPTON-ON-SEVERN, TEWKESBURY and ASHCHURCH

WEEK DAYS ONLY (Second class only)

February 1961

Miles		am	am	S am		pm	pm	pm	pm
—	Upton-on-Severn .. dep	7 57	..	..	..	1 30	..	..	5 45
2	Ripple	8 3	..	..	..	1 34	..	..	5A57
5½	Tewkesbury .. { arr	8 9	..	..	..	1 42	..	..	6 3
	dep	8 11	8 53	1110	....	1 43	4 156	6	
7¼	Ashchurch .. .. arr	8 16	8 58	1115	..	..	1 48	4 20	6 11

Miles		am	am	S am	pm	pm	pm
—	Ashchurch .... dep	8 35	9 25	...	1130	2 20	5 10	6 20
1¾	Tewkesbury .. { arr	8 40	9 30	.	1135	2 25	5 15	6 25
	dep	....	....	....	1137	..	5 17	..
5½	Ripple	....	....	•	1147	..	5 25	..
7¼	Upton-on-Severn .. arr	....	....	....	1152	..	5 29	..

A Arr 5 49 pm   S Saturdays only

58.   Moving to the 1864 station in about 1951, we see a Great Malvern to Ashchurch service hauled by no. 43373, an ex-MR class 3F 0-6-0. While the coach was suitable for propelling, tender engines were not so equipped. Passenger service north of Upton-on-Severn was withdrawn on 1st December 1952 and south thereof on 14th August 1961. (Lens of Sutton coll.)

59.   Running round its solitary coach on 1st May 1956 is 0-4-4T no. 58071. Most trains terminated here by that time. Access to the engine shed was via the line on the right, also the goods yard which closed on 2nd November 1964. The signal box closed on 17th December 1961, the line from Ashchurch having been singled in 1958. (H.C.Casserley)

60.   Two photographs from 10th July 1959 survey this rural outpost comprehensively. This panorama includes two BR trailers and the photographer's Hillman 10. North of the station was Tewkesbury Tunnel (420yds), Three Arches Viaduct (33yds) and River Avon Viaduct (62yds). Parts of these can still be seen. (H.C.Casserley)

61.   The 6.20pm from Ashchurch was worked by no. 43337 and it waits for a train signalled in the other direction, the late running 5.45 from Upton. The locomotive will then retire to the shed. (R.M.Casserley)

62.   The spacious accommodation for gentlemen is near the massive telegraph pole carrying all messages to the station from the railway telephone system. No. 41900 is working to Upton-on-Severn, not long before the service ceased. (Millbrook House)

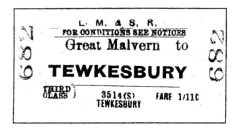

L. M. & S. R.

FOR CONDITIONS SEE NOTICES

Great Malvern   to

TEWKESBURY

THIRD CLASS   3514(S)   FARE 1/11C
TEWKESBURY

RIPPLE

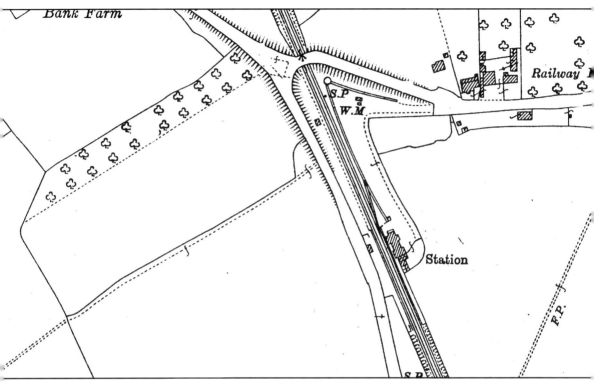

XVI. The 1928 survey does not include the crossover or signal box, as these were removed in 1910. A wagon turntable was a novel way of extending a siding.

63. Class 3F no. 43373 stands with the 5.45pm from Upton-on-Severn on 8th March 1956, as the light was fading. This train was scheduled to wait here from 5.49 to 5.57, which gave the photographer time to record the rear of it. (R.M.Casserley)

64.   He had time to enjoy the architectural joys of the fine building, despite the LMS placing one of their hawkseye signs rather thoughtlessly. The goods yard remained in use until 1st July 1963. (R.M.Casserley)

65.   The station is in the distance in this view from the 1930s; both bridges appear in the two previous photos. The down line had been given over to wagon storage in 1922. (R.S.Carpenter coll.)

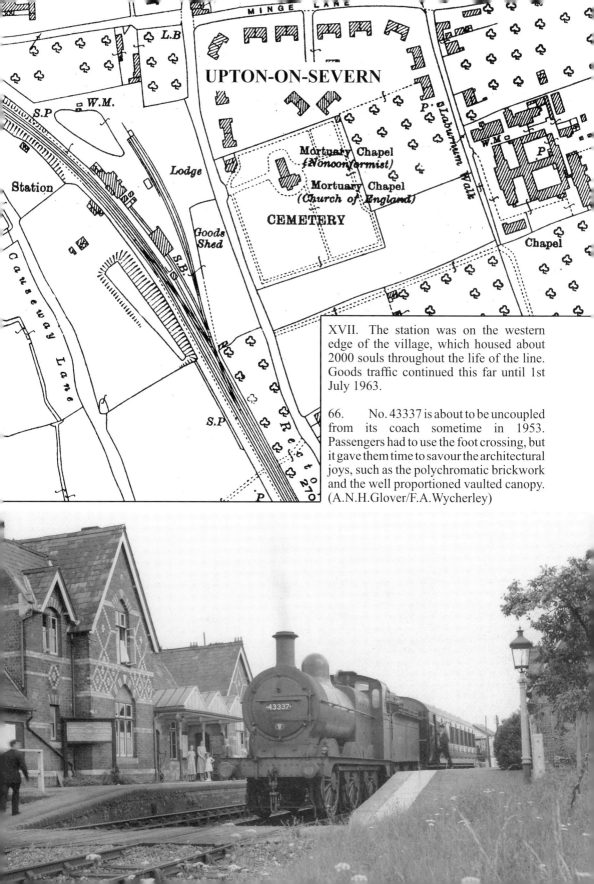

MINGE LANE

UPTON-ON-SEVERN

L.B

S.P

W.M.

Station

Lodge

Goods
Shed

S.B.

Mortuary Chapel
(Nonconformist)

Mortuary Chapel
(Church of England)

CEMETERY

Laburnum Walk

W.M.

P.

Chapel

Causeway Lane

S.P.

S.P.

Reservoir 270

P.

XVII. The station was on the western edge of the village, which housed about 2000 souls throughout the life of the line. Goods traffic continued this far until 1st July 1963.

66.   No. 43337 is about to be uncoupled from its coach sometime in 1953. Passengers had to use the foot crossing, but it gave them time to savour the architectural joys, such as the polychromatic brickwork and the well proportioned vaulted canopy. (A.N.H.Glover/F.A.Wycherley)

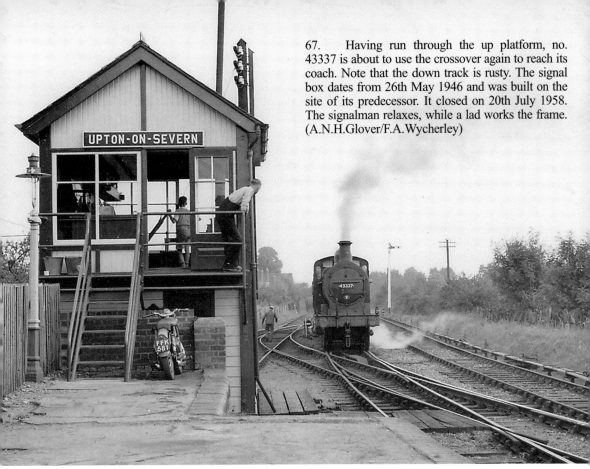

67. Having run through the up platform, no. 43337 is about to use the crossover again to reach its coach. Note that the down track is rusty. The signal box dates from 26th May 1946 and was built on the site of its predecessor. It closed on 20th July 1958. The signalman relaxes, while a lad works the frame. (A.N.H.Glover/F.A.Wycherley)

68. Now enjoy the remaining fenestrated ridge tiles, the complexity of the chimney stacks and the stylish barge boards. (R.S.Carpenter)

69. The MR bi-directional signal survived to be photographed in 1958. Almost a mile to the south were Lode Sidings; four were laid down for the Air Ministry in 1938. They were close to the 145yd long River Severn Viaduct. (D.Ibbotson/R.S.Carpenter)

70. Our final look at this idyllic location is in August 1960. It had been a terminus since 1952 and in its final years had departures at 7.57am and 5.45pm, Mondays to Fridays, while on Saturdays there was an extra one at 1.30pm. (H.B.Priestley/Milepost 92½)

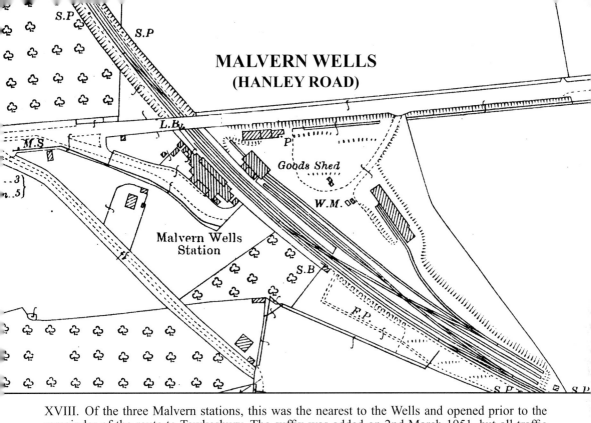

MALVERN WELLS
(HANLEY ROAD)

XVIII. Of the three Malvern stations, this was the nearest to the Wells and opened prior to the remainder of the route to Tewkesbury. The suffix was added on 2nd March 1951, but all traffic ceased on 1st December 1952. Running across the 1927 map is the B4209, so numbered in 1919.

71.   The prospective passenger's perspective was recorded on 3rd September 1917. The station house is on the left and both buildings have stone quoins and mullions, adding to their appeal. (R.K.Cope/R.S.Carpenter)

72.   Photographed on the same day in the goods yard was one of Mr. Kirtley's well tanks, with a carefully composed group of railwaymen. The number was painted for the myopic. Completed in about 1870, it ran until 1927. (R.K.Cope/R.S.Carpenter)

73.   The vaulting was more extensive on the platform side, but well proportioned. Curiously, there was no canopy on the up side. The foot crossing is close to the bridge in this 1939 view. The GWR's Malvern Wells station was about one mile to the north. (Stations UK)

74.   Other features of charm were the double gables of the up waiting room and its chimney appearing as part of the attached goods shed. The signal box was only four years old when photographed in 1949; it had a 20-lever frame and was in use until line closure in 1952. (H.C.Casserley)

75.   A fine panorama from 1951 includes the other door of the goods shed, together with the short-lived suffix and the beautiful backdrop of the enchanting Malvern Hills. (R.M.Casserley coll.)

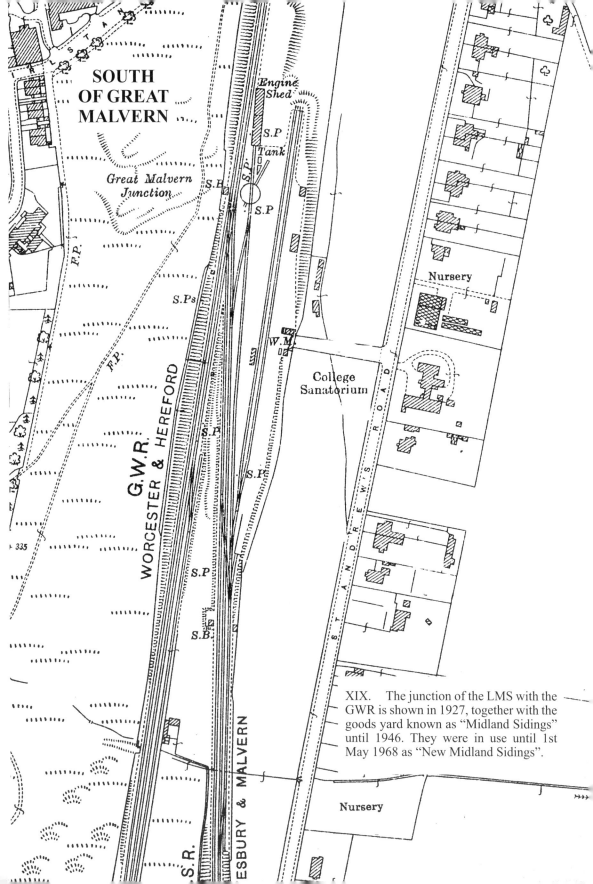

SOUTH OF GREAT MALVERN

Engine Shed

S.P

Tank

S.B.

S.P.

S.P.

Great Malvern Junction

S.B.

F.P.

F.P.

S.Ps

W.M.

College Sanatorium

G.W.R.
WORCESTER & HEREFORD

S.P.

S.P.

S.P.

S.P.

S.B.

S.R.

ESBURY & MALVERN

Nursery

S T A N D R E W S R O A D

Nursery

+ 335

XIX. The junction of the LMS with the GWR is shown in 1927, together with the goods yard known as "Midland Sidings" until 1946. They were in use until 1st May 1968 as "New Midland Sidings".

76.   A single coach train is signalled for the Ashchurch route sometime in the 1930s. The signal box was named "Malvern & Tewkesbury Junction" and was GWR property. The LMS "Malvern Sidings" box was further south (see map). The former closed on 14th November 1954 and the latter on 24th October of that year; it had 12 levers. Thereafter, access to the sidings necessitated a double reversal from a new connection from the down goods loop on the former GWR route. (W.A.Camwell)

77.   No. 6914 *Langton Hall* speeds towards Hereford in about 1946, with Great Malvern in the background. The turntable pit is clearer, but the ex-MR engine shed had closed on 14th September 1931, although the table was used at least until 1939. The first shed was replaced in 1883 and extended in about 1898. (J.Scott-Morgan coll./R.S.Carpenter)

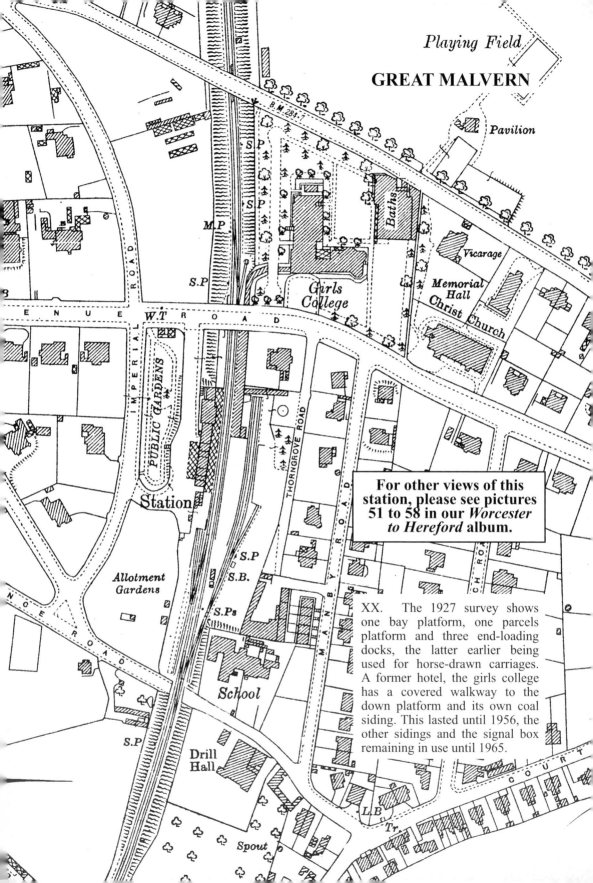

Playing Field

GREAT MALVERN

Pavilion

B.M. 281.7

S.P

S.P

M.P

S.P

Baths

Vicarage

Girls College

Memorial Hall

Christ Church

ENUE

W.T ROAD

IMPERIAL ROAD

PUBLIC GARDENS

THORNGROVE ROAD

MANBY ROAD

CH ROAD

For other views of this station, please see pictures 51 to 58 in our *Worcester to Hereford* album.

Station

Allotment Gardens

S.P

S.B.

S.Ps

NOE ROAD

School

XX. The 1927 survey shows one bay platform, one parcels platform and three end-loading docks, the latter earlier being used for horse-drawn carriages. A former hotel, the girls college has a covered walkway to the down platform and its own coal siding. This lasted until 1956, the other sidings and the signal box remaining in use until 1965.

S.P

Drill Hall

L.B

Tr

COURT

Spout

78. A train for Ashchurch stands at the up platform in 1949, ex-LMS 2-6-2T no. 40116 having run round the coach using the down line. The main lines were not so obstructed after 1952, when the service was withdrawn. (J.Moss/R.S.Carpenter)

79. The Ashchurch train was often moved to the bay to await departure time. No. 58051 will leave at 6.30pm on 10th May 1952, with limited visibility, due to the coal. In the left background is the passage to the down platform. (T.J.Edgington)

Cleeve Station

CLEEVE

XXI. The station was situated on an unclassified road between Stoke Orchard and Bishops Cleeve. About 2½ miles south of Cleeve, a station called Swindon was opened on 26th May 1842. Fortunately it closed on 1st October 1844, before causing too much confusion.

80. A snap from 1923 has poor focus, but shows the small size of the station building. Both it and the goods yard were closed on 20th February 1950. (Stations UK)

81.   This southward panorama is probably from the 1950s and includes a rare example of an MR cast iron urinal. (Lens of Sutton coll.)

82.   Seen in the 1960s, the signal box was in use from 19th November 1944 until 17th February 1969. It had a 20-lever frame. The goods yard tracks had been lifted in 1963. The white painted station house remains standing today. (Lens of Sutton coll.)

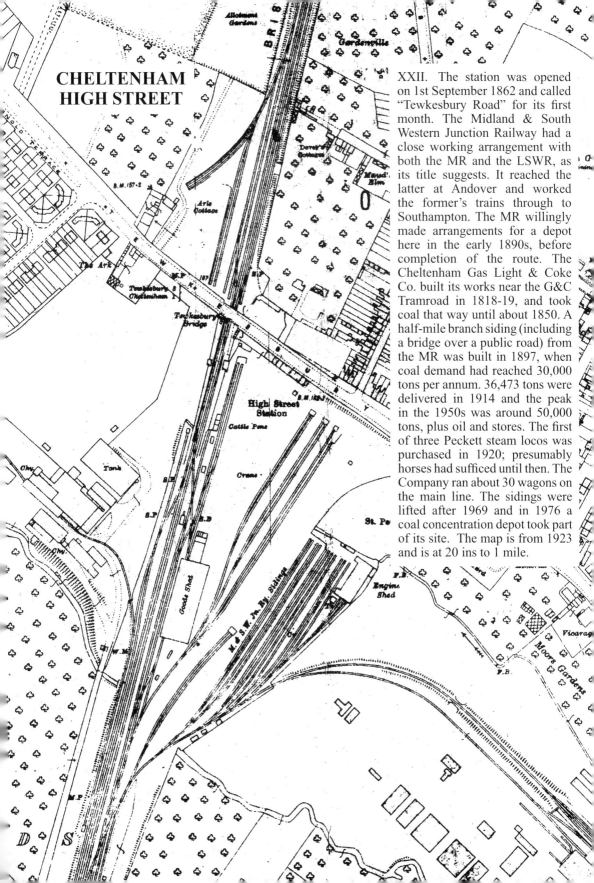

CHELTENHAM HIGH STREET

XXII. The station was opened on 1st September 1862 and called "Tewkesbury Road" for its first month. The Midland & South Western Junction Railway had a close working arrangement with both the MR and the LSWR, as its title suggests. It reached the latter at Andover and worked the former's trains through to Southampton. The MR willingly made arrangements for a depot here in the early 1890s, before completion of the route. The Cheltenham Gas Light & Coke Co. built its works near the G&C Tramroad in 1818-19, and took coal that way until about 1850. A half-mile branch siding (including a bridge over a public road) from the MR was built in 1897, when coal demand had reached 30,000 tons per annum. 36,473 tons were delivered in 1914 and the peak in the 1950s was around 50,000 tons, plus oil and stores. The first of three Peckett steam locos was purchased in 1920; presumably horses had sufficed until then. The Company ran about 30 wagons on the main line. The sidings were lifted after 1969 and in 1976 a coal concentration depot took part of its site. The map is from 1923 and is at 20 ins to 1 mile.

83.   This southward view is from about 1933 and features (centre) the ex-MR goods shed (now a listed structure) and the 27-lever signal box. The latter closed on 25th November 1968 and the goods yards on 3rd January 1966. Remnants of the passenger station are evident; this had closed on 1st July 1910. The up goods loop (right) was created from a siding in 1942 and was still in use in 2005. (Mowat coll./Brunel University)

84.   The former MSWJR shed is seen in 1936; the company had ten sidings to the left of it, plus two short ones. The first single-road wooden shed was completed in 1893, and was replaced by this structure in 1911, which remained in use until December 1935. The allocation in 1923 comprised six 4-4-0s, five 0-6-0s, two 2-4-0s and one 4-4-4T. There had been a total of ten locomotives back in 1902. (W.A.Camwell)

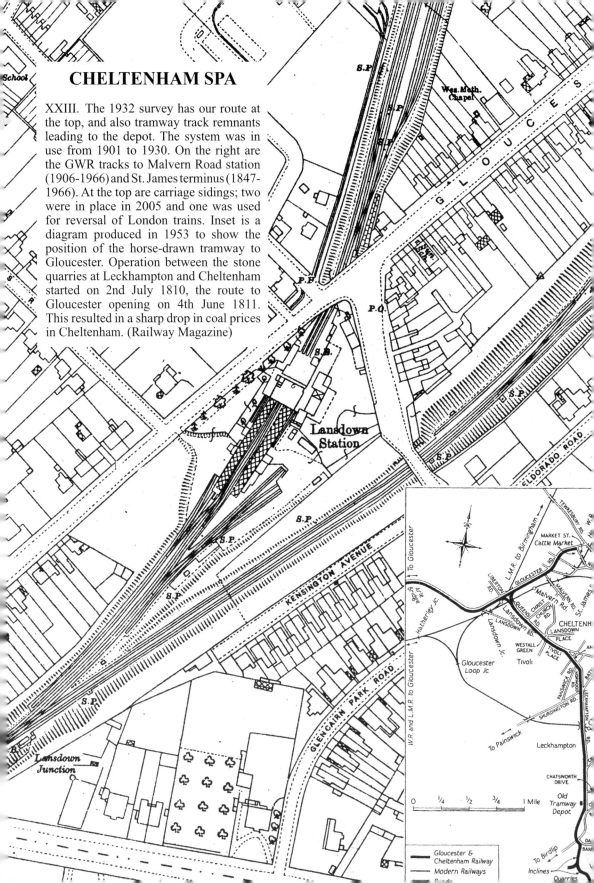

CHELTENHAM SPA

XXIII. The 1932 survey has our route at the top, and also tramway track remnants leading to the depot. The system was in use from 1901 to 1930. On the right are the GWR tracks to Malvern Road station (1906-1966) and St. James terminus (1847-1966). At the top are carriage sidings; two were in place in 2005 and one was used for reversal of London trains. Inset is a diagram produced in 1953 to show the position of the horse-drawn tramway to Gloucester. Operation between the stone quarries at Leckhampton and Cheltenham started on 2nd July 1810, the route to Gloucester opening on 4th June 1811. This resulted in a sharp drop in coal prices in Cheltenham. (Railway Magazine)

85.　　Thought to date from the 1870s, this view of a southbound MR train features the early roof stanchions which proved to be too close to the platform edge for safety. The station had the suffix "Lansdown" from 1925 to 1966. (P.Q.Treloar coll.)

86.　　It was initially demanded that the station must be "a respectable distance from the centre of the town". This has been a nuisance ever since, but now one can walk along the GWR trackbed for a mile or more. A bold statement about the importance of the railway was made architecturally. While the Spa went into decline, the intellectual status of the town rose with the expansion of prestigious seats of learning. (H.C.Casserley coll.)

87.　　The main building is in the background in this 1949 view of no. 20216, a type designed by Mr. Johnson for the MR in 1876. It is on one of the two short dock lines. (W.Potter/P.Q.Treloar)

88.　　A 1956 northward view reveals that MR vaulting had replaced the original overall roof. The short siding on the left would have been a convenient place to unload coal for station use. (R.M.Casserley)

89.　　Southbound on 1st May 1956 is no. 90448, an ex-WD 2-8-0 formerly numbered 63127. The distant signal is indicating a clear run through to Lansdown Junction. The bay platform had been used by Andover and Southampton trains for many years, mainly 1891 to 1923. These were operated by the MSWJR. (H.C.Casserley)

For further photos of the Cheltenham area, please see *Stratford-upon-Avon to Cheltenham* and *Cheltenham to Andover*.

90.   At the north end of the up platform on 13th May 1961 was ex-GWR no. 4109. Such an interloper would have been unlikely before 1958, when the station fell into the Western Region. (H.C.Casserley)

91.   This 28-lever box operated at the north end of the down platform from 28th June 1891 until 23rd January 1966. The next box south was at Lansdown Junction. The roofs were reclad with corrugated asbestos in 1971. (R.J.Essery/R.S.Carpenter)

92.　　Southbound on 16th September 1975 are china clay empties from Staffordshire, bound for Cornwall. In charge is no. D1048 *Western Lady*. In the foreground is the route to Stratford-upon-Avon, which was in use until 1977. Note that the down platform had been greatly lengthened following the removal of the sidings in 1965. (T.Heavyside)

93.   Three photographs from 4th November 2005 show a clean and smart station, which was very busy. The London service had been greatly enhanced in 2002 with ten direct trains on weekdays, instead of four. All but one of the splendid Grecian columns had been destroyed in 1961. (V.Mitchell)

94.   A view from the east entrance shows that there are two separate footbridges to the ticket hall. There are ramps to both platforms and there are trains direct to about half of England, plus the capitals of Wales and Scotland. (V.Mitchell)

95.   The unusual relationship of the footbridges to the roofs is the purpose of this northward photograph. A class 158 DMU is working the 08.35 from Gloucester to Worcester. The 08.57 departure to Nottingham provided the only direct service of the day to Bromsgrove. (V.Mitchell)

LANSDOWN JUNCTION

XXIV. This map overlaps no. XXII and our route to Gloucester is at the left border. The Banbury line opened in this area in 1881 and carried traffic until 1962. Major changes took place in 1942 when the route was quadrupled from here to Gloucester.

96.　　On the right is the line from Cheltenham Malvern Road and we witness ex-LMS 4-6-0 no. 45712 leaving Lansdown, its down and bay platforms being visible in the background. The year is about 1961. Part of the 1942 retaining wall is on the left. (A.W.V.Mace/Milepost 92½)

97.   Looking from the other side of the same bridge, we see the simple junction, with the Gloucester line on the right. Out of sight is the connection between the routes, which formed a triangle from 1906 until 1956. Few passenger trains used it, but the Newcastle-Cardiff service was a notable exception. The spur joined at Hatherley Junction, where there was a 47-lever signal box until 20th November 1966. (Mowat coll./Brunel University)

THROUGH TRAINS BETWEEN

NEWCASTLE and CARDIFF, BARRY, and SWANSEA.

Page Ref.		Week Days. mrn A	Sundays. mrn		Page Ref.		Week Days. mrn A	Sundays. mrn A
830	Newcastle (Central) .....dep.	9 30	....			Swansea (High Street) ..dep.	7 40	10 25
	Durham (Main) .... ″	9 58	....			Neath (General).......... ″	7 57	10 45
831	Darlington (Bank Top).. ″	10 34	....			Briton Ferry (West)...... ″		10 52
	Northallerton............ ″	10 56	....		67	Port Talbot (General) .. ″	8 7	11 1
705	York .... ″	11 45	....		71	Pyle .... ″		11 16
	Hull (Paragon)........dep.	10 40	....			Bridgend .... ″	8 30	11 30
932	Goole............ ″	11 12	....			Llantrisant .... ″		11 48
	Thorne (North)........ ″	11 24	....					aft
	Doncaster (Central) .. ″	11 47	....			Cardiff (General) ....arr.	9 30	12 5
911	Rotherham & Masboro'. ″	aft 12 13	....		89	Barry..............dep.	9 5	
	Sheffield (Victoria).....arr.	12 24	....			Barry Docks .... ″	9 11	
350-54	Sheffield (Victoria)...... dep.	1 0	9 15		71	Cardiff (General)).........dep.	9 40	12 25
	Nottingham (Victoria)... ″	1 55	10 15		73	Newport (High Street) ... ″	10 0	12 52
851	Leicester (Central) ...... ″	2 28	10 50			Chepstow .... ″	10 27	
855	Rugby (Central) .... ″	2 55	11 18		74	Gloucester(GW)[hampton ″	11 3	
	Woodford and Hinton.... ″		11 41			Cheltenham (Sth) & Leck– ″	11 17	
	Banbury (Bridge Street).. arr.	3 30	11 55		130	Bourton-on-the-Water ... ″	11K47	
106	Oxford (G.W.) .... ″		12 30			Stow-on-the-Wold .... ″	11K52	
15	Swindon .... ″		2 0				aft	
	Chipping Norton .... ″	4 0 8			20	Chipping Norton........ ″	12K9	2 50
130	Stow-on-the-Wold .... ″	4 25				Swindon .... ″		3 40
	Bourton-on-the-Water ... ″	4 31			102	Oxford (G.W.) .... ″		4 8
	Cheltenham (Sth) & Leck– ″	4 59				Banbury (Bridge Street).. arr.	12 38	4 16
72, 74	Gloucester(GW)[hampton ″	5 10				Banbury (Bridge Street).. dep.	12 44	4 50
66	Chepstow................ ″	5 57			844	Rugby (Central) .... arr.	1 16	4 50
72	Newport (High Street) ... ″	6 21	3 49		848	Leicester (Central) ...... ″	1 38	5 11
	Cardiff (General) .... ″	6 47	4 12		845	Nottingham (Victoria) ... ″	2 8	5 43
89	Barry Docks .... arr.	7 15				Sheffield (Victoria) 849.. ″	3 3	6 39
	Barry .... ″	7 20			906	Sheffield (Victoria).......dep.	3 18	
	Cardiff (General) ....dep.	6 55	4 28		932	Doncaster (Central) .....arr.	3 50	
	Llantrisant............. arr.		4 46			Hull (Paragon)........ ″	4 45	
64	Bridgend................ ″	7 54	5 6		704	Sheffield (Victoria).......dep.	3 12	
66	Port Talbot (General) ... ″	8 14	5 27			York ....arr.	4 13	
	Briton Ferry (West)...... ″		5 35		825	Northallerton............ ″	5 19	
	Neath (General)......... ″	8 23	5 44			Darlington (Bank Top) .. ″	5 49	
	Swansea (High Street) .. ″	8 42	6 0		827	Durham (Main) .... ″	6 15	
						Newcastle (Central)...... ″	6 33	

A Through Carriages from Hull (Paragon) to Cardiff, Barry, Swansea and vice versa.   **D** Stops to set down from Rugby and beyond on informing the Guard at Banbury.   **K** Stops to take up for Rugby and beyond on notice being given at the Station.   ☞ Through Restaurant Cars between Newcastle, Cardiff, Barry, and Swansea.

XXV.   Bradshaw July 1929

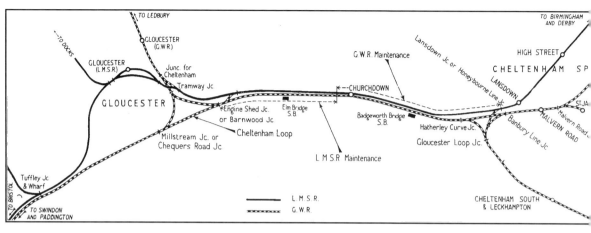

XXVI. The quadrupling involved major civil engineering work and the provision of the two additional tracks, on the south side mostly. Contrary to the diagram, the old up main line became the up relief and old down line the new up main. The two companies carried out the work on their halves of the route, thus the signals had different quadrants of action. However, the GWR had to concede over track designation. Only the fresh intermediate signal boxes are marked.

98.   The signal box shown on the map was replaced by this one on 26th July 1942. It had 102 levers and lasted until 12th November 1977. The photo is from 16th September 1975 and is from the same viewpoint as the previous picture. No. 47105 is heading the 08.48 Cardiff to Leeds. A down goods loop was all that was left of the quadruple track by that time. (T.Heavyside)

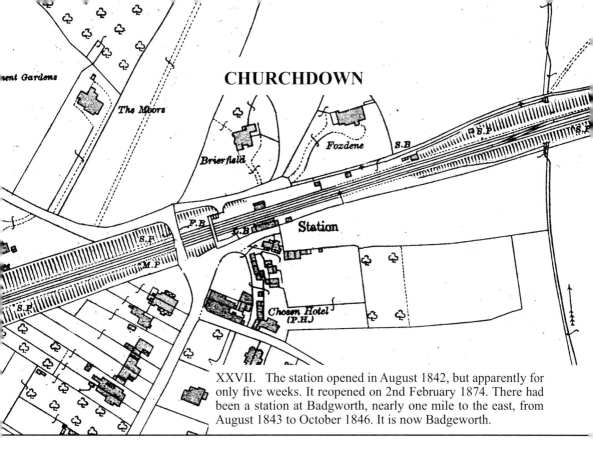

CHURCHDOWN

XXVII. The station opened in August 1842, but apparently for only five weeks. It reopened on 2nd February 1874. There had been a station at Badgworth, nearly one mile to the east, from August 1843 to October 1846. It is now Badgeworth.

99.   A train bound for Gloucester arrives in about 1905. A personal weighing machine backs onto the west wall; 1d in the slot would give you the figure. The local population rose from 989 in 1901 to 7075 in 1961. (Lens of Sutton coll.)

100.   A panorama eastwards in May 1961 reveals that the MR up waiting shelter survived the 1942 alterations. The 45-lever signal box came into use on 28th June of that year, its predecessor being largely obscured on the left of the previous view. (H.C.Casserley)

101.   Creeping along the down relief line on 12th May 1961 is ex-GWR 4-6-0 no. 6807 *Birchwood Grange*. The new lines were opened in stages in 1942 and four new signal boxes, plus 13 gantry signals, had to be provided. (H.C.Casserley)

102.   Platform faces on the relief lines were not opened until March 1944. These tracks were taken out of use in stages in 1966-67 and the signal box closed on 26th February 1967. On the up relief line on 6th August 1960 is 0-6-0 no. 44296 piloting 2-10-0 no. 92137. The station closure took place on 2nd November 1964. (G.Adams/M.J.Stretton)

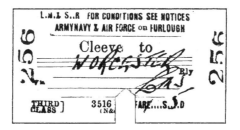

EAST OF GLOUCESTER

103.   Reference to the last diagram will show that Elm Bridge was one of the fresh intermediate boxes in 1942. The GWR managed to provide one of traditional style. Ex-GWR 2-6-0 no. 6394 passes it southbound on 7th April 1964. Its 12 levers were not used after May 1965. (M.A.N.Johnston)

XXVIII.   This diagram indicates the position of the original tramway in relation to the railways of 1953. The junction names have varied: Barnwood Junction was Engine Shed Junction until 26th May 1968 and Tramway Junction was Horton Road Junction from the same date. The earlier Barnwood Junction was near the engine shed - see next map. (Railway Magazine)

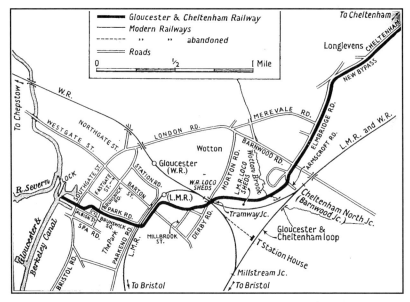

104. The location of T Station House is indicated on the diagram. All trains used the station marked WR initially. After the triangular junction was created, the GWR opened T Station, so called because it formed a T junction, by means of a turntable, which allowed through coaches to and from Gloucester to link with their London-Cheltenham services. It was in use in 1847-51 and photographed in 1954. Demolition followed. (A.J.G.Dickens/C.G.Maggs)

105. On the northern part of the triangle and approaching Tramway Junction on 5th September 1948 is 0-6-0 no. 44185 with a local train from Birmingham. This side of the triangle was quadrupled in 1940-41 and the intermediate signal box called Barnwood Junction was closed. At its eastern end was Engine Shed Junction box which had 105 levers. (Millbrook House)

106.   No. 3604 was recorded with a short freight on the same day obscuring the former GWR engine shed. In the background is Gloucester Cathedral, and Passenger Station signal box, seen clearer in pictures 113 and 117. (Millbrook House)

107.   The 1895 MR Barnwood engine shed was on the north side of the triangle. Although rectangular in outline, it functioned as a roundhouse with a 50ft central turntable. This and the next picture were taken on 8th September 1949. (H.C.Casserley)

108. In the background is the ramp for wagons going to the coal stage built by the MR; also included are the signals for Cheltenham North Junction. Taking coal on 29th April 1950 is no. 3062, one of the 2F type introduced by the MR in 1878. The GWR engine shed was behind the camera, beyond Horton Road. The LMS shed was coded 22B in 1935 and 85E by the Western Region (later it was 85C). Closure was on 4th May 1964. (H.C.Casserley)

109. The level crossing for Horton Road is on the site of the tramway crossing and was fitted with lifting barriers at about the time that the present panel box opened on 25th May 1968. This faces the lines to Bristol (right). The 50-lever Tramway Junction box was to the left of the front loco from 1896 until that time. Nos 20157 and 20172 are arriving from the Cheltenham direction on 16th September 1975. (T.Heavyside)

GLOUCESTER

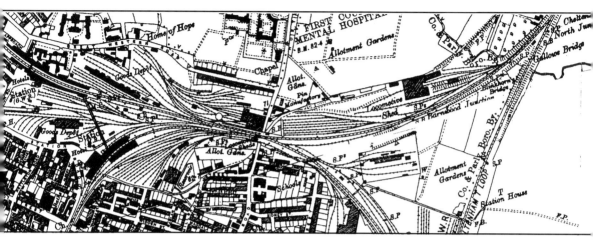

XXIX. Top left on this 1922 edition is the GWR station and the line to South Wales. Below it is the MR goods depot and to the right of that is the MR station, which is connected to that of the GWR by a very long footbridge. On the right is T Station House and below it the GWR lines converge towards Gloucester South Junction. The Cheltenham Loop (right) did not exist between 1872 and 1901, when it was reopened for goods. It was traversed by through passenger trains from 1st July 1908.

110.   The MR goods depot was a little to the south of the site of its first passenger station, which was a terminus. The Tuffley Loop (lower left on the map) was opened on 22nd May 1854, following the abandonment of broad gauge to Bristol. This avoided the need for a fresh engine on long distance trains reversing here. Reversal was ended by the opening of a station on the loop on 12th April 1896. No. 1295 heads the last train to leave the old terminus on the previous day. (LGRP)

111.   The 1896 station was known as "Gloucester Midland" until it became "Eastgate" in 1951. Standing at its centre through platform in about 1913 is 4-2-2 no. 614, southbound. Above the wide staircase on platform 1, a sign advises TO TRAINS TO THE WEST OF ENGLAND BRISTOL BATH BOURNEMOUTH AND TO THE GREAT WESTERN STATION. GWR destinations were of no interest to their rival. It became "Central" in 1951. (R.S.Carpenter coll.)

112.   More of the footbridge can be seen across the background of this westward view, probably from the 1920s. The graceful MR 4-2-2 is no. 676 and it is passing the 1896 40-lever Gloucester Passenger Station box. Behind the train is the up bay platform, numbered 1. (R.M.Casserley coll.)

113.   Taken from further down the same platform, this photograph of ex-LMS 4-4-0 no. 40523 is from 8th September 1949. The locomotive is bringing empty stock out of the carriage sidings. (H.C.Casserley)

114.   A fine picture from platform 1 in April 1955 features the other MR staircase and a sign advising WAY OUT AND TO THE GREAT WESTERN STATION, seven years after the GWR had vanished. Paddington-Cheltenham services used platform 2 in 1964-75, but reversal has been necessary at all other times for trains calling at Gloucester. (R.M.Casserley)

115.   Arriving at platform 3 with the 5.45pm Birmingham to Bristol on 11th July 1956 is ex-LMS 4-4-0 no. 41195. EASTGATE was added below the running-in board and below it can be seen Gloucester Goods Junction box, which had a 36-lever frame in use until March 1968. In the far distance is Tramway Junction box. (H.C.Casserley)

116. "The Devonian" is hauled northwards by ex-LMS 4-6-0 no. 45651 in this view from the late 1950s. A composite coach of the same origin is in the bay platform. More of the lengthy footbridge is evident. (Millbrook House)

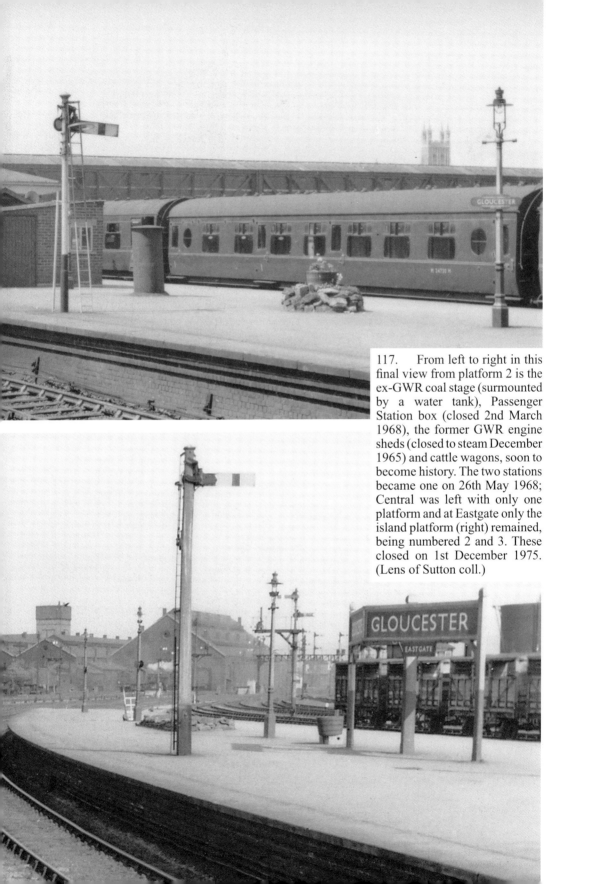

117.   From left to right in this final view from platform 2 is the ex-GWR coal stage (surmounted by a water tank), Passenger Station box (closed 2nd March 1968), the former GWR engine sheds (closed to steam December 1965) and cattle wagons, soon to become history. The two stations became one on 26th May 1968; Central was left with only one platform and at Eastgate only the island platform (right) remained, being numbered 2 and 3. These closed on 1st December 1975. (Lens of Sutton coll.)

118.   We include the former Central platforms as they were used by all trains from Cheltenham after 1st December 1975. Trains in opposite directions used two parts of one long platform, as they did in the 1840s at this and other GWR principal stations. No. 46028 is about to use the crossover with the 11.45 Cardiff to Newcastle on 16th September 1975. Work is in progress on the left on a new station building. (T.Heavyside)

119.   A westward panorama in July 1977 from the mean shelter at the east end of the passenger platform shows the revised position and direction of the crossover. The 1968 alterations involved removal of the footbridge and the up platform being dedicated to parcels, as seen here. The main entrance is in the distance, fine for the fit in good weather. That end of the platform was numbered 2. (D.Thompson)

120.   The up platform became No. 3 in 1984 following erection of a new, but roofless, footbridge and restoration of passenger services to it. This is the featureless, but functional building in July 2005. Most important was that the train frequencies and destinations were better than ever before, despite many long distance trains bypassing the station on the eastern part of the triangle. (V.Mitchell)

Middleton Press albums on this area, showing their special features
Gloucester to Bristol - MR Dock Lines
Gloucester to Cardiff - GWR Dock Lines
Hereford to Worcester - Ledbury Branch
Swindon to Gloucester - Golden Valley

MP Middleton Press

EVOLVING THE ULTIMATE RAIL ENCYCLOPEDIA

Easebourne Lane, Midhurst, West Sussex.
GU29 9AZ Tel:01730 813169

www.middletonpress.co.uk   email:info@middletonpress.co.uk

A-0 906520 B-1 873793 C-1 901706 D-1 904474

OOP Out of Print at time of printing - Please check current availability **BROCHURE AVAILABLE SHOWING NEW TITLES**